MW01199384

NEW BEGINNINGS

A Guide For New Believers Taking The

First Steps on Their Christian Journey

Bob Wright

Edited By

Kaylyn Wright

Website restoremenow.org
Email: info@restoremenow.org

Contents

Introduction

For those new to the Christian faith, I highly recommend diving into the enriching pages of "New Beginnings." This exceptional guide will illuminate your path and provide a deeper understanding of the Christian life. As you embark on your spiritual journey, laying a solid foundation is crucial, and this book will undoubtedly help you do just that. From exploring the importance of the Christian community to understanding concepts such as water baptism, prayer, and spiritual growth, "New Beginnings" offers a step-by-step guide that will save you months, if not years, of struggling to find your place in the body of Christ. You will also delve into topics like baptism in the Holy Spirit, cultivating generosity, and discovering your spiritual gifts. With its empowering insights and practical guidance, I am confident that this book will ignite a passion and purpose within you as you embrace your faith. Don't hesitate any longer - take the first step towards unlocking your incredible spiritual potential by diving into the pages of "New Beginnings. "I have also included a prayer for individuals who desire to accept Jesus Christ as their Lord and Savior. Whether you are a new believer or want a fresh view of the first steps, "New Beginnings" is an excellent read.

The first step in becoming a Christian is to accept Christ as Lord and Savior. Jesus told Nicodemus, "You must be born again" (John 3:3).

Being born again spiritually is the key that unlocks the spiritual part of man. It opens the door to a relationship with God through his Son, Jesus Christ.

(John 3:16) says, For God so loved the world, that he gave his only begotten Son, that whosoever believeth in him should not perish, but have everlasting life.

In (John 3:3-5) Jesus explains that being born again is the only way to enter the kingdom of God. The new birth is necessary to become a new creation in Christ. (Romans. 3:23) tells us, "All have sinned and come short of the glory of God. God sent his Son into the world through an incredible act of love to pay the penalty for our sins so we could be forgiven.

If you have not accepted Jesus Christ as Savior, I invite you to say this prayer with me:

"Dear Heavenly Father, I come to you in the name of your Son, Jesus Christ. You said in (John 6:37), the one who comes to You, you would not turn away. In (Romans 10:10), your word says that if I confess with my mouth the Lord Jesus and believe that you raised Him from the dead, I would be saved. "I believe that Jesus is the Son of God and that He was raised from the dead. Through His death on the cross, my sins have been forgiven. I also believe that He was raised from the dead to justify me. I confess Him as my Lord and Savior." Your word also says, 'With the heart, man believes unto righteousness.' I believe with all my heart that I am a born-again Christian and have received a new life in God through Christ. Thank you, Lord Jesus, for coming into my heart. Amen!"

Congratulations if you said this prayer! You are ready to continue reading this book. I pray it will guide you and help you grow in Christ.

Welcome to the beginning of a remarkable journey that surpasses the boundaries of the ordinary and propels you into the extraordinary. As you stand at the threshold of your new life in Christ, it's essential to understand that the decision you've made marks not only a change in belief but a profound transformation of your entire existence.

In the days, weeks, and months ahead, expect to encounter the warmth of divine love and the gentle guidance of a Shepherd who knows you intimately. Your new life in Christ is not merely a set of religious rituals and rules but a dynamic relationship with a living God. You are embarking on a journey towards a deeper understanding of your identity and God's love. A journey will bring a sense of purpose beyond anything you've experienced. Your new life in Christ is a departure from the old, marked by a profound shift in perspective and priorities. The values that once dictated your choices will yield to the transformative power of God's Word. While challenges may arise, remember that your newfound faith equips you with resilience and strength that surpasses human understanding.

Expect a renewed mind — a mind that seeks truth, embraces compassion, and finds wisdom in Christ's teachings. Any baggage of guilt and shame that may have burdened your past is exchanged for the liberating grace that flows from the cross. Your new life invites you to walk in freedom, unencumbered by the chains of sin, and to experience the joy of forgiveness Christ offers.

The transition from your old life to the new may present challenges, but be assured that God's grace is sufficient for every step. Managing this change requires a deliberate commitment to prayer, the study of God's Word, and fellowship with other believers. Surround yourself with a community of believers who uplift and support your newfound journey, encouraging you in times of doubt and celebrating with you in times of triumph.

Navigating relationships from your past, especially those that may be toxic, demands discernment and courage. While your love for others remains steadfast, prioritize your spiritual well-being. Establish healthy boundaries and seek God's guidance in determining the role of these relationships in your new life. Remember, as you grow in faith, your transformed life becomes a testament to the power of God's love. One of the most powerful aspects of your walk with Christ is that of walking in love. It's not just a suggestion; it's a way of life that deepens your connection with God and is a compelling witness to those around you.

"The essence of love is beautifully captured by the Apostle John in (1 John 4:7-8.) "Beloved, let us love one another, for love is from God, and whoever loves has been born of God and knows God. Anyone who does not love does not know God because God is love."

When you choose to walk in love, you mirror the very nature of God. God is love; as His children, expressing love becomes a tangible way of manifesting His presence in your life. Others will be drawn to the warmth and kindness that emanates from a heart rooted in love.

Love has the extraordinary ability to break down barriers and dissolve preconceived notions. Approaching others with genuine love and compassion creates a space for open dialogue. People are more receptive to the message of Christ when it is delivered in an atmosphere of love.

Your actions often speak louder than words. By consistently demonstrating love in your interactions with others—whether through acts of kindness, forgiveness, or understanding—you become a living testimony to the transforming power of Christ. This form of "lifestyle evangelism" can have a profound impact on those around you.

Jesus, our ultimate example, showed love to the marginalized, the broken, and even those who opposed Him. As you model Christ in your new Christian walk, allow people to see God's love in you. A Love that transcends circumstances and challenges, leading the broken and lost to Christ. When a community of believers embodies love, it becomes an inviting space for those seeking something deeper. When believers walk in love, it fosters an environment where unbelievers can experience the warmth of Christian fellowship, making them more receptive to becoming part of God's family.

In your newfound journey of faith, remember that walking in love is not just a means to an end; it is a beautiful expression of your relationship with God and a compelling way to share His love with the world. As you love others genuinely and unconditionally, you become a beacon of light, pointing others toward the source of that love—our Savior, Jesus Christ.

For this reason, always approach your new life humbly, recognizing that growth is a continuous process. The difficulties you may encounter are opportunities for God's grace to abound and for your character to be refined. Trust in the promise that God, who began this good work in you, will complete it.

As you embark on your Christian journey, know you are not alone. The God who calls you is faithful, and His love will guide you through every step of your new life in Christ. Taking the necessary steps toward spiritual growth involves becoming the person God intended you to be. In the next chapter, you will be guided through a step-by-step process that will help you learn how to become a dynamic person of God. By the time you reach the end of this book, you will be positioned to reach your full potential, growing spiritually in ways you never thought possible.

CHAPTER 1

The Power of Community:

Joining A Strong Christian Network

Joining together with a community of believers holds deep significance for every Christian. Attending church and forming connections with fellow Christians goes beyond tradition or duty; it embodies a core aspect of the Christian belief, rooted in the teachings of Jesus Christ and demonstrated by the early church. In today's individualistic and isolated world, the value of Christians uniting in fellowship cannot be overstated. The importance of Christians attending church and connecting with other believers encompasses several foundational aspects of the Christian faith, each deeply rooted in biblical teachings and exemplified throughout Scripture.

Regular attendance at church provides a structured environment for believers to engage in worship, prayer, and the study of God's Word. In Hebrews 10:24-25), believers are encouraged to "consider how to stir up one another to love and good works, not neglecting to meet together, as is the habit of some, but encouraging one another, and all the more as you see the Day drawing near." This passage emphasizes the mutual edification and encouragement that occurs when believers gather together. Through corporate worship and fellowship, Christians are spurred on to deepen their relationship with God and to grow in their understanding of His truth.

Connecting with other believers in a local church setting provides a framework for accountability and spiritual support. (James 5:16) urges believers to "confess your sins to one another and pray for one another, that you may be healed." This practice of mutual accountability fosters humility, honesty, and transparency within the Christian community, creating a safe space for individuals to share their struggles, receive guidance, and experience healing and restoration.

Life's journey is often fraught with challenges, trials, and uncertainties. In times of need, the church serves as a source of comfort, encouragement, and practical support. (Galatians 6:2) instructs believers to "bear one another's burdens, and so fulfill the law of Christ." Through acts of service, compassion, and generosity, members of the church family come alongside one another, offering practical assistance and spiritual guidance during times of difficulty and hardship.

At the heart of the Christian faith lies the commandment to love one another as Christ has loved us (John 13:34-35). Gathering in fellowship allows believers to express this love in tangible ways through acts of kindness, hospitality, and sacrificial service. (Romans 12:10) exhorts believers to "love one another with brotherly affection. Outdo one another in showing honor." By prioritizing relationships and investing in the well-being of fellow believers, Christians embody the love of Christ and bear witness to His transformative power in their lives.

"Regularly attending church is vital for nurturing our spiritual health and keeping us strong, focused, and connected to Jesus; if we are not actively involved with a community of believers to support us, our spiritual lives will suffer. Just as an arm becomes useless when separated from the body, our spiritual lives also suffer without the support and connection of other believers. Without the guidance and fellowship of pastors and teachers, we are vulnerable to the attacks of Satan, who targets isolated believers. Fellowship with others is crucial for our spiritual growth and strength; it keeps us from becoming spiritually deficient and unable to overcome challenges in our lives.

(1 Peter 5:8) warns us to "Stay alert! Watch out for your great enemy, the devil. He prowls around like a roaring lion, looking for someone to devour.

Jesus never sent his disciples out alone, emphasizing the importance of functioning as a body under the guidance of the Holy Spirit. As a united body, we can overcome attacks from the enemy and grow into a powerful church able to reach the world with the good news of salvation through Jesus Christ. One of the ways to improve our spiritual growth and strength is by having fellowship with stronger Christians. Every day, we face temptations, and being around people who live a godly life can be helpful.

Gathering with other believers will also give us the courage and strength to remain faithful to our Lord Jesus Christ even when faced with resistance from unbelieving family members and friends. As we grow in our relationship with God through fellowship with other believers, unbelievers will see that the word of God is active and working in our lives. We are instructed to come together to worship God in the unity of the Spirit. This is a scriptural mandate that every believer should follow faithfully.

"When we gather to worship and praise God, we become a powerful force that can overcome anything together. This is because Jesus dwells in the midst of our praise. (Psalm 22:3) Our togetherness grants the opportunity to support and motivate one another, which is essential for spiritual growth." This kind of love and unity inspires others to come to Christ.

Attending church regularly has another important benefit. There, you will have access to a pastor and other trained teachers who can help equip you to serve in the kingdom. These teachers are dedicated to helping you discover your ministry gift. You will find their teachings valuable assets. Through their teaching and guidance, you will have the opportunity to discover where you are called to serve.

Coming together with other believers is a beautiful experience. Some of my most cherished memories have been at church services, where people accept Jesus Christ into their lives. It is a blessing to be part of a community that shares in each other's lives and provides love, prayers, and support to those in need within the church family.

Church is a great place to meet and connect with like-minded people. Having friends who share your faith is crucial. The Bible encourages us to surround ourselves with fellow believers who can offer support and encouragement on our journey with Christ.

(Proverbs 27:17) highlights the importance of having good friends who can help sharpen us, just like iron sharpens iron. Christian friends can play a crucial role in our lives, making us better in every way and providing a sense of belonging. As social beings, we naturally crave connection and community, and having a group of people who share our faith can provide us with the support we need. Additionally, our Christian family joins us in celebrating moments of joy and success in a way that non-believers may not understand.

Being a part of a Christian community helps us stay on track with our spiritual goals. When we spend time with people who prioritize their faith, we are likelier to do the same. We may be inspired to attend Church more regularly, read our Bibles more consistently, or pray more fervently. Observing our Christian friends actively practicing their faith encourages us to do the same.

If you don't have a group of Christian friends, consider joining a small group at your Church or attending a Bible study. Investing in your spiritual health will lead to personal growth and meaningful relationships that last a lifetime. This step can be a catalyst for a deeper understanding of your faith and a stronger connection with God.

Let's summarize some of the benefits of being a part of a Christian community.

Spiritual Growth: Being a part of a Christian community helps in spiritual growth. You can learn about the Bible, pray together, and discuss important spiritual issues with others. This creates a foundation for growth and helps to deepen your relationship with God.

Support: Being a part of a Christian community can be a great source of support when going through difficult times. You can receive emotional, spiritual, and material support from Christian friends who care about you and want to help you.

Accountability: Being part of a Christian community involves having individuals who will keep you accountable. It's essential to surround yourself with people who will guide you when you stray and offer gentle correction when you make mistakes.

Encouragement: When you are a part of a Christian community, you can be encouraged by others who share your faith. This can be especially helpful when you are feeling discouraged or facing challenges.

Fellowship: Being part of a Christian community provides a profound sense of belonging. It's a place where individuals with shared beliefs and values come together, fostering deeper friendships and a strong sense of inclusion.

Service: Being part of a church is a unique opportunity to engage in meaningful activities that contribute to the well-being of others and the community at large. From outreach programs to volunteering initiatives, there's always something happening within the church that allows individuals to make a positive impact. This sense of purpose and the opportunity to serve others not only ignites a passion within members but also inspires and motivates them, making their involvement in the church deeply fulfilling.

In essence, being part of a church is more than just attending services—it's about actively participating in a community that celebrates faith, fellowship, and the joy of serving others. Being part of a church community is an exhilarating experience that goes beyond mere attendance at services. It's about being embraced into a tight-knit family, where individuals come together, united by their unwavering faith, to worship, learn, and grow together. Every step taken is filled with an electrifying sense of belonging, strengthened by the shared purpose that binds everyone together. In a church, there's an indescribable energy pulsing through the air, fueled by the unique blend of backgrounds, experiences, and talents that each member brings to the table. It's like watching a symphony unfold before your eyes, as every believer contributes their own beautiful notes to create a harmonious masterpiece.

CHAPTER 2

Preparing For Baptism

What you need to know

Congratulations on your decision to take another step of faith on your incredible journey! You are standing at the threshold of an extraordinary life-changing experience: Following Christ's example in water baptism. Water baptism is the next step on your Christian journey and represents your commitment to follow Jesus Christ.

In this chapter, we will explore the beauty and significance of water baptism. We will unpack the deep roots of this sacred act found in the Scriptures and understand how it serves as a gateway to a new life in Christ. I aim to make this journey enlightening and exciting and, above all, to strengthen your walk with the Savior.

Water baptism holds great significance in the Christian faith. (Matthew 3:13) Says Jesus was baptized by John the Baptist in the Jordan River.

(Matthew 28:19) Jesus commanded his disciples to "Go therefore and make disciples of all the nations, baptizing them in the name of the Father and of the Son and of the Holy Spirit."

Water baptism is a command that applies to all Christians. It serves as a visible expression of their faith and commitment to Christ. This practice is rooted in the teachings of Jesus, who himself was baptized. By undergoing water baptism, believers are obeying Christ's command to baptize people in the name of the Father, Son, and Holy Spirit. Beyond mere obedience, baptism holds profound symbolic significance. As the new Christian is immersed in the water, it represents the burial of their old, sinful self, mirroring the death of Jesus on the cross. Emerging from the water symbolizes the resurrection to a new life in Christ, illustrating the transforming power of faith.

This declaration of faith publicly reinforces a Christian's commitment to Christ and fosters a sense of unity among the community of believers.

Moreover, water baptism is a powerful initiation into the broader Christian community. It marks the beginning of the new believer's journey within the body of Christ, emphasizing their connection with fellow followers and their shared identity. This public aspect is crucial for spiritual growth, as baptism signifies a personal transformation and integration into a network of believers who can provide encouragement, guidance, and shared fellowship on the Christian journey. Baptism by water is a significant milestone in the spiritual journey of new Christians. It embodies elements of obedience, symbolism, and mutual bonds that serve as building blocks for their spiritual foundation and growth. The apostles practiced water baptism. For instance, in Acts 2:38, Peter instructed the people to "Repent, and let every one of you be baptized in the name of Jesus Christ for the remission of sins; and you shall receive the gift of the Holy Spirit."

Following the sermon, (Acts 2:41) says, "Then those who gladly received his word were baptized; and on that day about three thousand souls were added to them."

Water baptism is a spiritual act that signifies the cleansing of sin and the start of a new life in Christ. It represents the burial of your old life and the resurrection into a new life in Christ.

(II Corinthians 5:17) "Therefore, if anyone is in Christ, he is a new creation; old things have passed away; behold, all things have become new."

The Biblical method of baptism is a complete water immersion, symbolizing burial. John baptized Jesus in the river Jorden. God's word does not support baptism by merely having water sprinkled on your head, as some practice.

(Mark 1:10) "And immediately, coming up from the water, He saw the heavens parting and the Spirit descending upon Him like a dove." Jesus must have been submerged in water to come up out of it. John's use of a river indicates immersion, not sprinkling.

It is essential to obey Jesus' commandment and be baptized in water by immersion as soon as possible after accepting him as your Savior. Water baptism is an outward expression of inward change and is necessary for all Christians.

Baptism is a public declaration of one's faith and symbolizes the washing away of sins. It testifies to a new life received through belief in Christ. Additionally, through baptism, we join with a community of believers by participating in a tradition that has been practiced for centuries.

Apostle Paul explains the purpose of water baptism in ... (Romans 6:3-7) NLT:

(Vs.3) Or do you not know that as many as were baptized into Christ Jesus were baptized into his death?

(Vs.4) Therefore we have been buried with him through baptism into death, so that just as Christ was raised from the dead through the glory of the Father, we too may live a new life.

(Vs.5) For if we have become united with him in the likeness of his death, we will certainly also be united in the likeness of his resurrection.

(Vs.6) We know that our old man was crucified with him so that the body of sin would no longer dominate us so that we would no longer be enslaved to sin.

(Vs.7) For someone who has died has been freed from sin.

Paul emphasizes that baptism is far more than just a symbolic gesture. It has a profound spiritual impact, granting us the ability to overcome the power of sin. Therefore, baptism frees us from sin's grip on our lives.

To summarize, Christians should follow Christ's example and be baptized for several reasons. I will list just a few.

1. It Is A Commandment Of Jesus Christ

(Matthew 28:19), Jesus commands his disciples to "go and make disciples of all nations, baptizing them in the name of the Father and of the Son and of the Holy Spirit." As followers of Christ, we should obey his commands, and water baptism is one of them.

2. It Is A Public Declaration Of Faith

Water baptism is a public declaration of our faith in Jesus Christ. By being baptized, we declare to the world that we have accepted Jesus as our Lord and Savior and are committed to following him.

3 It Symbolizes Our Death And Resurrection With Christ

(Romans 6:4) tells us that "we were buried therefore with him by baptism into death, so that, just as Christ was raised from the dead by the glory of the Father, we too might walk in newness of life." Water baptism symbolizes our death to our old way of life and our resurrection to a new life in Christ.

4. It is a step of obedience

As Christians, we are called to obey God's commands. Water baptism is one of the first steps of obedience we take as new believers, and it sets us on the path to a life of following Christ.

5. It is a part of our spiritual growth

Water baptism is a significant milestone in our spiritual development. It is a step of faith that furthers growth in our relationship with God and to become more like Christ. It is a reminder of the grace and mercy we have received through our salvation and a recognition of our commitment to live a life that honors God.

CHAPTER 3

Unlocking the Door to Heaven

The Importance of Prayer

As a Christian, having a fulfilling life requires a strong and unbreakable bond with God, which is achieved through consistent and intimate prayer. However, this can be challenging as it demands dedication and discipline on our part. Yet, regular communication with Him is paramount in nurturing and strengthening our faith. It also plays a vital role in our spiritual growth and connection with the Lord. Maintaining a regular prayer routine keeps any doubts or uncertainties at bay and deepens our relationship with Christ. This allows us to freely communicate our struggles and triumphs, ask for help, express our needs, and give thanks for His endless grace and blessings. After all, prayer is simply talking to God and building a closer connection with Him.

Developing a meaningful prayer life is an ongoing process that requires a commitment to take time out of our busy lives to talk with God.

You will encounter various styles and techniques as you establish your prayer life. Familiarizing yourself with these different forms of prayer and understanding when to use them can help you maintain your focus and intentions.

Here are some examples of prayers that may be helpful for specific situations.

The Prayer of Thanksgiving:

Let's look at the Prayer of Thanksgiving. It is a conversation with God that emphasizes gratitude. Expressing thankfulness adds depth and richness to your relationship with God. Picture it as a heartfelt letter to the One who has showered you with countless blessings, both seen and unseen. In this prayer, you express gratitude for what God does and who He is — a loving and ever-present Father.

So, what is the prayer of thanksgiving? It's your chance to pause, reflect, and acknowledge the goodness that permeates your life. It's about appreciating the ordinary miracles, the daily provisions, and the moments of joy God graces you with. It says, "Thank you, God, for your love, guidance, and the countless gifts you bestow upon me.

(1 Thessalonians 5:16-18) NIV:

"Rejoice always, pray continually, give thanks in all circumstances; for this is God's will for you in Christ Jesus."

Make giving thanks a constant reminder of God's abundance and faithfulness in your newfound faith. Form a habit of recounting your blessings, recognizing each as a testament to God's provision.

One biblical story that beautifully illustrates the power of thanksgiving is the account of Jesus feeding the multitude, found in all four Gospels: (Matthew 14:13-21), (Mark 6:30-44), (Luke 9:10-17), and (John 6:1-15).

In this story, Jesus is teaching and healing a vast crowd gathered to hear Him. The disciples became concerned about the multitude's hunger as the day wore on. Sensing their need and moved with compassion, Jesus asked Philip, "Where shall we buy bread for these people to eat?" (John 6:5) NIV:

Philip, perplexed by the enormity of the task, replied that it would take more than half a year's wages to buy enough bread to feed such a large crowd. Another disciple, Andrew, spoke up, mentioning a boy with five barley loaves and two fish, but he questioned how far that would go among so many people.

Undeterred by the apparent lack, Jesus instructed the disciples to have the people sit down in groups of fifty on the grass. Taking the loaves and fish, He looked up to heaven, blessed the food, and began breaking the loaves, which the disciples distributed to the people. Miraculously, everyone ate as much as they wanted, and when they had eaten their fill, the disciples collected twelve basketfuls of leftovers.

This miraculous provision was a demonstration of Jesus' divine power and a profound act of thanksgiving. Jesus didn't just provide food to satisfy physical hunger; He provided an abundance that exceeded all expectations. In giving thanks for the meager offering of the loaves and fish, Jesus transformed them into a feast that nourished the bodies and souls of thousands.

This story reminds us that Thanksgiving is not just about expressing gratitude for what we have but also recognizing God's abundant provision in every circumstance. Even when faced with scarcity or impossibility, we can trust God's faithfulness to provide for our needs and fill us with His abundance. As we offer thanks to God for His provision, we open ourselves to receive even more incredible blessings so we can share them generously with others.

For the new believer, this prayer is a continual source of joy and a reminder of God's love and provision. When you experience it, your outlook changes, and you start to feel satisfied and grateful for the beautiful things around you. So, my dear friend, on this journey of faith, let your prayers echo with gratitude, and may the practice of thanksgiving be a cornerstone in building a resilient and joy-filled life.

The Prayer of Praise:

Praise is a beautiful way to express your genuine appreciation and acknowledgment of God's greatness. It is not about fancy words or elaborate expressions but a heartfelt recognition of God's goodness, power, and love. When you pray the prayer of praise, you say something like, "God, you are awesome, and I praise you for being my God and for your power and ability to save and deliver me."

The story of Paul and Silas praising God in prison is a powerful demonstration of the power of praise and worship. It's found in (Acts 16:16-40).

In this account, Paul and Silas were on a missionary journey in Philippi, preaching the Gospel and sharing the message of salvation. One day, as they were going to the place of prayer, they were accosted by a slave girl who was possessed by a spirit of divination. She had brought her owners a great deal of money through fortune-telling.

Paul, filled with the Holy Spirit, commanded the evil spirit to come out of her, setting her free from bondage. However, this act of deliverance angered the girls' owners, who realized that their source of income had been taken away. They seized Paul and Silas and dragged them before the authorities, accusing them of disturbing the peace and advocating customs unlawful for Romans to practice.

The magistrates, yielding to the pressure of the crowd, ordered Paul and Silas to be stripped and beaten with rods before being thrown into the inner prison, their feet fastened securely in stocks. Despite their unjust treatment and the harsh conditions of their confinement, Paul and Silas did not despair. Instead, they turned to God in prayer and praise.

At midnight, while Paul and Silas were praying and singing hymns to God, an earthquake suddenly shook the foundations of the prison, causing the doors to fly open and everyone's chains to come loose. The jailer awakened from sleep and, seeing the prison doors open, was filled with fear, assuming that the prisoners had escaped. He drew his sword, intending to take his own life rather than face the consequences of their escape.

But Paul, recognizing the jailer's desperation, called out to him, reassuring him that they were all still there. The jailer, trembling with fear and awe, fell down before Paul and Silas and asked them what he must do to be saved. They replied, "Believe in the Lord Jesus, and you will be saved — you and your household. Filled with newfound faith, the jailer took Paul and Silas into his home, where they shared the Gospel with his family, and they were all baptized. The jailer then tended to their wounds, and they shared a meal, rejoicing in the salvation that had come to his household.

This remarkable event not only saved the jailer and his family but also testified to the power of praise and worship in the midst of adversity. Despite their suffering, Paul and Silas remained steadfast in their faith. They found strength in praising God, ultimately bringing about a miraculous intervention that led to the spread of the Gospel and the transformation of lives.

(Psalm 150:1-6)

"Praise ye the LORD. Praise God in his sanctuary: Praise him in the firmament of his power. Praise him for his mighty acts: Praise him according to his excellent greatness. Praise him with the sound of the trumpet: Praise him with the psaltery and harp"

You acknowledge and honor God's greatness in your life by praising Him. "Greater is he that is in you, than he that is in the world" (1 John 4:4). We should give God praise for His incredible love and blessings even in the lowest points of our lives. The prayer of praise keeps our faith fixed on His ability to deliver and restore during challenging times. Praise also keeps us focused on His delivering power even when facing seemingly impossible situations.

(Matthew 19:26) "With men this is impossible, but with God all things are possible"

The Prayer of Confession:

The prayer of confession is having an honest conversation with God about our shortcomings and mistakes. It is not about self-condemnation but rather an acknowledgment of our imperfections and a genuine desire to receive His forgiveness and transformation. It simply says, "God, I messed up and need your help." Imagine it as a candid talk with a trusted friend, admitting when you've gone off course. Confession is essential to the Christian journey, allowing you to come as you are without pretense. It's not about listing every detail of your mistakes but recognizing the need for God's mercy and guidance. The Bible encourages believers to confess their sins to find forgiveness and healing.

David gives us a beautiful example of the prayer of confession. The story of King David's prayer of confession in Psalm 51 provides us with a glimpse into the heart of a man who recognizes his need for God's mercy and forgiveness. It's deeply personal and introspective. King David penned this Psalm after he was confronted by the prophet Nathan regarding his sin with Bathsheba and the subsequent murder of her husband, Uriah.

In (Psalm 51), David pours out his soul before God, acknowledging his transgressions and pleading for cleansing and restoration. The Psalm begins with a heartfelt plea:

"Have mercy on me, O God,

according to your unfailing love.

according to your great compassion

blot out my transgressions.

Wash away all my iniquity

and cleanse me from my sin." (Psalm 51:1-2), NIV:

David acknowledges the gravity of his sins, confessing, "For I know my transgressions and my sin is always before me." In verse 3, he recognizes that his wrongdoing is not merely a violation of human law but a betrayal of God's trust and a defilement of his soul.

Despite the weight of his guilt, David appeals to God's character of steadfast love and mercy. He pleads for spiritual renewal, asking God to create a pure heart and renew a steadfast spirit within him (Psalm 51:10). He longs to be restored to a right relationship with God, acknowledging that only God can bring about true transformation and renewal.

David's prayer of confession is not merely a request for forgiveness but a profound expression of repentance and contrition. He acknowledges that God desires truth in the innermost being and recognizes the need for a genuine change of heart (Psalm 51:6). He surrenders himself entirely to God's judgment, acknowledging that his sin is ultimately against God alone (Psalm 51:4).

David expresses his confidence in God's willingness to forgive and restore as the Psalm progresses. He anticipates the joy of salvation and the opportunity to proclaim God's righteousness and praise (Psalm 51:12-15). He offers the sacrifice of a broken spirit and a contrite heart, recognizing that these are the offerings that God truly desires (Psalm 51:17).

In conclusion, Psalm 51 serves as a powerful testament to the transformative power of confession and repentance. Through David's prayer, we are reminded of God's boundless mercy and grace, which are available to all who humbly come before Him with contrite hearts. David's example challenges us to examine our lives, confess our sins before God, and trust in His unfailing love and forgiveness.

The Prayer of Petition:

The prayer of petition is a sincere conversation with God where you bring your wants, needs, and desires to Him, knowing that the One who knows you intimately is listening to every word.

Simply put, the prayer of petition says, "God, I need Your help, guidance, and provision." It is an honest expression of your vulnerabilities and a declaration of your dependence on a caring God. You can imagine it as a safe space where you lay down your burdens and ask for divine intervention.

(Matthew 7:7–11) "Ask, and it will be given to you; seek, and you will find; knock, and it will be opened to you."

One of the Bible's most famous stories of a prayer of petition is the story of Hannah, found in (1 Samuel 1:1-20).

Hannah was a woman who longed for a child, but she was unable to conceive. This was a source of great sorrow and shame for her, especially in a society where a woman's worth was often measured by her ability to bear children. Despite her pain, Hannah remained faithful to God and poured out her heart in prayer.

Year after year, Hannah accompanied her husband, Elkanah, to the Tabernacle at Shiloh to worship and offer sacrifices. On one such occasion, Hannah was deeply distressed and wept bitterly as she prayed to the Lord, pleading for a child. In her anguish, she made a vow to God, saying, "Lord Almighty, if you will only look on your servant's misery and remember me, and not forget your servant but give her a son, then I will give him to the Lord for all the days of his life, and no razor will ever be used on his head." (1 Samuel 1:11)

Hannah's prayer was a heartfelt petition born from her deepest desires and sorrows. She poured out her soul before God, laying bare her longing for a child and her willingness to surrender him to the Lord's service if her petition were granted. Hannah trusted God's faithfulness and power to answer her prayer despite her pain and uncertainty.

The high priest Eli, who was present at the tabernacle, observed Hannah praying silently, her lips moving but no sound coming out. Mistaking her anguish for drunkenness, Eli rebuked her, but Hannah respectfully explained her situation and poured out her heart before him.

Upon hearing her petition, Eli blessed Hannah, saying, "Go in peace, and may the God of Israel grant you what you have asked of him." (1 Samuel 1:17)

Encouraged by Eli's words and strengthened by her faith, Hannah left the Tabernacle with a new-found sense of peace and hope in her heart.

In due time, God remembered Hannah and answered her prayer. She conceived and gave birth to a son named Samuel, meaning "heard by God." True to her vow, Hannah dedicated Samuel to the Lord's service from his earliest days, bringing him to the Tabernacle at Shiloh once he was weaned to serve under the priest Eli.

Hannah's story is a powerful testament to the efficacy of prayer and the faithfulness of God to answer the petitions of His people. It reminds us that even in our deepest sorrows and most desperate moments, we can turn to God in prayer, trusting in His love and provision to fulfill our deepest longings according to His perfect will.

As you navigate your early steps in faith, embrace the prayer of petition as a vital part of your relationship with God. Don't be afraid to present your concerns, dreams, and challenges to Him. It's not about having the right words but sharing your heart openly. The prayer of petition cultivates trust and deepens your faith in God's willingness to help us in our time of need.

(Matthew 7:7–11) "Ask, and it will be given to you; seek, and you will find; knock, and it will be opened to you."

Whether in moments of joy or uncertainty, know that you can turn to God with your needs. This prayer will become a source of comfort and strength and a reminder that you are never alone on your path of faith. We should always talk to our heavenly Father about our needs.

(Philippians 4:6) "Be anxious for nothing, but in everything by prayer and supplication, with thanksgiving, let your requests be made known to God."

Throughout the Bible, we see that before and after Christ's birth, men and women went to God with their needs. Like them, God encourages us to bring our problems, hurts, and needs to Him.

The Prayer of Intercession:

The prayer of intercession is a way to bring the needs of others before God. It's like being an advocate for someone else, expressing genuine care and concern on their behalf. It's asking, "God, please help another person. Consider it a conversation where you lift the needs of friends and family by asking God to intervene on their behalf. It's not about eloquence; it's about compassion. The prayer of intercession is grounded in the belief that God listens and responds to our requests for others.

In (Acts 12:5-12) there is a beautiful example of the prayer of intercession.

In the city of Jerusalem, where the Christians gathered and the devout prayed, a group of believers clung to their faith despite the persecution that loomed over them. Among them was Peter, an apostle of Jesus Christ.

As the story unfolds, Herod Agrippa, the ruler of Judea, sought to please the Jewish leaders by arresting Peter and throwing him into prison. The night before Peter was to stand trial, he found himself bound in chains, guarded by soldiers, and surrounded by darkness. But the believers did not lose hope even in the depths of despair. They fervently interceded for Peter's deliverance, their hearts united in faith, and their voices lifted in supplication.

Meanwhile, Peter slept soundly in his cell, unaware of the prayers being offered on his behalf. Suddenly, a radiant light pierced through the darkness of the prison, and an angel of the Lord appeared before Peter, gently nudging him awake. With a touch of divine intervention, the chains that bound Peter fell away, and the angel instructed him to rise and follow.

In a daze, Peter obeyed, his steps guided by the hand of God. Passing by the guards unnoticed, they made their way through the iron gates of the city, which swung open of their own accord. It was a miraculous escape orchestrated by the Almighty, a testament to His power and His faithfulness to those who trust in Him.

As Peter emerged into the streets of Jerusalem, he realized that God had delivered him from the clutches of death. Overwhelmed with gratitude, he made his way to the house of Mary, the mother of John Mark, where the believers had gathered in fervent prayer for his release.

When Peter knocked on the door, a servant girl named Rhoda answered, her eyes widening in disbelief at the sight of him standing before her.

Rushing to inform the others, she left Peter standing outside, still incredulous at the miracle that had just unfolded.

Soon, the believers emerged from their prayers, their faces glowing with joy and astonishment as they beheld Peter, safe and sound, in their midst. Their prayers had been answered in a way they could scarcely have imagined, reaffirming their faith in God's power to do the impossible.

With hearts overflowing with thanksgiving, the believers praised God for His deliverance, rejoicing in His mercy and His unfailing love. And Peter, emboldened by his miraculous escape, continued to proclaim the gospel with renewed zeal, knowing that the Lord was with him every step of the way.

This Bible story encourages believers to intercede for one another. This kind of prayer fosters a sense of community and shared responsibility for one another. Intercessory prayer will become a natural part of your spiritual routine as you develop your prayer life. It is a way to actively show love and support for others, acknowledging that we are all on this journey together.

(I Timothy 2:1-4) "Therefore I exhort first of all that supplications, prayers, intercessions, and giving of thanks be made for all men, for kings and all who are in authority, that we may lead a quiet and peaceable life in all godliness and reverence. For this is good and acceptable in the sight of God our Savior, who desires all men to be saved and to come to the knowledge of the truth."

The Prayer of Agreement:

The prayer of agreement is uniting with our brothers and sisters in Christ and agreeing on specific prayer needs.

Jesus taught us about the prayer of agreement as seen in (Matthew 18:19-20) "Again I say to you that if two of you agree on earth concerning anything that they ask, it will be done for them by My Father in heaven."

There may be times when you need the agreement of other Christians concerning a need in your life. Nothing is more special than God's people praying in agreement for each other in the name of our Lord Jesus Christ. At its essence, the prayer of agreement emphasizes the power of a unified purpose. It is more than a mere joining of voices; it's a convergence of hearts, minds, and spirits in faith. This unity amplifies the strength of individual prayers, creating a collective plea that resonates with the will of God. In a world often characterized by division, this prayer fosters a beautiful sense of oneness among believers, transcending differences for a higher, shared purpose.

Jesus Himself highlighted the prayer of agreement and its effectiveness. When believers come together, their collective faith forms a channel through which God's blessings and interventions flow. (Matthew 18:19-20) serves as a timeless reminder of the authority bestowed upon united believers, underscoring the impact of their agreement in the spiritual realm.

Whether seeking healing, guidance, provision, or interceding for others, the power of agreement lies in the shared conviction that God is faithful to His promises. This prayer model encourages believers to clearly articulate their requests, believing that God's response is certain and generous as they stand together.

Our agreement in faith releases God's anointing and brings breakthroughs and victory to our lives.

The shared burden becomes a shared victory, emphasizing the importance of the power of agreement in the body of Christ.

In summary, Prayer is a source of strength and spiritual renewal. We grow stronger in faith and deeper in God's love by praying daily. Daily prayer equips you to deal with the struggles that come your way and enables you to face tests and trials with overcoming faith. Remembering, the victory that God promised is yours!

Prayer has numerous benefits for those who practice it regularly. First and foremost, prayer is talking with God and seeking His guidance and strength. Scientific studies have proven that Prayer helps reduce stress and anxiety and provides peace and calm.

Studies have also shown that Prayer has physical benefits, such as reduced blood pressure and heart rate and improved overall health and well-being. Finally, prayer provides a sense of purpose and meaning in life as we seek to align our will with God's will and live a life of service and love for others.

Dear Friend,

Thank you for choosing "New Beginnings" to help guide you on your journey of exploration and growth. If you've enjoyed the insights, encouragement, and guidance offered in "New Beginnings," please take a moment to leave a review. Your words have the power to help others decide to embark on this transformative journey.

To share your review, Scan The QR Code Below. Your feedback is a gift, and I am genuinely grateful for your time and consideration.

CHAPTER 4

Growing In Faith

Through a Study of God's Word

Our faith is built upon the understanding that the Bible is God's holy and inspired word.

It is the foundation of our faith and the source of our knowledge about God, His plan for salvation, and how we should live as His followers. The Bible is not just another book; God's living and active word transforms lives and brings us into a deeper relationship with Him.

Living a Christian life can be challenging. As believers, we are called to follow Christ and obey His word, which can sometimes be challenging. We may face persecution, temptation, trials, and other obstacles that make staying on the right path difficult. However, we must remember that we are not alone in our struggles. God is with us every step of the way.

This Book of the Law shall not depart from your mouth, but you[a] shall meditate in it day and night, that you may observe to do according to all that is written in it. For then you will make your way prosperous, and then you will have good success. Joshua 1:8 NKJV:

Joshua 1:8 holds profound implications for the everyday Christian walk. It offers timeless wisdom that transcends historical context and speaks directly to the challenges and aspirations of contemporary believers. At its core, this verse underscores the fundamental importance of cultivating a deep, intimate relationship with God through studying and applying His Word.

In the hustle and bustle of modern life, it's easy to become overwhelmed by competing priorities and distractions. Yet, like Joshua standing on the brink of the Promised Land, we, too, are called to navigate the complexities of life with unwavering faith and courage. The command to meditate on God's law day and night resonates with believers today, inviting us to carve out intentional moments of reflection and communion with God amidst the demands of our daily routines.

In practical terms, Joshua 1:8 challenges us to prioritize spiritual disciplines such as prayer, Bible study, and worship as foundational pillars of our Christian walk. Just as athletes diligently train their bodies for peak performance, so must we train our minds and hearts in the truths of Scripture. It's not enough to merely skim the surface of God's Word; true transformation occurs when we immerse ourselves deeply in its teachings, allowing them to permeate every aspect of our lives.

Moreover, the promise of success and prosperity articulated in Joshua 1:8 speaks to the holistic well-being of the believer. While the world may define success as wealth, fame, or power, the Christian understanding of success is rooted in obedience to God's will and alignment with His purposes.

As a result of our obedience and commitment to the Word, all the things the world seeks after are added to us. By faithfully following God's Word, we can experience the richness of His blessings — peace, joy, fulfillment, and the assurance of His presence in every circumstance. Therefore, during life's challenges and uncertainties, let us cling to the timeless counsel of Joshua 1:8.

We find strength and guidance in the Bible, Which is a source of wisdom and comfort for believers. By relying on God's power and grace, we can overcome any challenge and live a fulfilling and purposeful life as a follower of Christ.

As Seen above, The Bible is more than a collection of stories and teachings from the past; it is a living and active book that speaks to us today. In (2 Timothy 3:16-17) We read, "All Scripture is God-breathed and is useful for teaching, rebuking, correcting and training in righteousness, so that the servant of God may be thoroughly equipped for every good work." The Bible is the primary way God reveals Himself to us. Through its pages, we learn about His character, plan for salvation, and will for our lives. We gain knowledge about Jesus Christ through the Bible, the living Word of God.

(John 1:1) In the beginning was the Word, and the Word was with God, and the Word was God.

God's word is also our defense against Satan's lies and attacks. In Ephesians 6:17, we read that the Word of God is the sword of the Spirit, which we use to defend ourselves against his schemes. By knowing and studying the Bible, we can recognize and resist the lies and temptations that Satan sends our way and drive us off course.

The Bible is not just a book of knowledge but a source of spiritual nourishment and growth.

(1 Peter 2:2) Like newborn babies, you must crave pure spiritual milk so that you will grow into a full experience of salvation. Cry out for this nourishment, [3] now that you have had a taste of the Lord's kindness. God's word nourishes our inner man and is essential for our spiritual growth and development as believers.

Reading the word of God enlightens us about His character and love for us. We also learn about our sinfulness and our need for forgiveness. As we read and study the Bible, the Holy Spirit works in us to transform us into the person we were destined to become. In (Romans 12:2) we read that we should "not conform to the pattern of this world but be transformed by the renewing of our mind." God's word is the primary way that our minds are renewed and transformed by the Holy Spirit.

Moreover, the Bible is a transformative tool that guides us in developing a profound relationship with God. As we immerse ourselves in His Word, we not only gain a deeper understanding of Him but also begin to feel His presence in our lives. In (John 15:7), Jesus assures us, "If you remain in me and my words remain in you, ask whatever you wish, and it will be done for you." This promise is a testament to the incredible power and blessings that come with growing in faith through the Bible.

Applying God's Word to Our Daily Lives

Reading and studying the Bible is not enough; we must also apply its teachings to our daily walk. (James 1:22-25) tells us that we should not just listen to the Word of God but also do what it says. The Bible is not just a book of knowledge with historical facts; it is a book of wisdom that teaches us how to live in a way that honors God and blesses others.

One way to apply the Bible to our daily lives is through meditation. In (Psalm 1:2-3) we read that the blessed person meditates on God's Word day and night and becomes like a tree planted by water streams that yield fruit in season. By meditating on God's Word, we assimilate its teachings and apply them to our daily lives.

Another way to incorporate the Bible's teachings into our everyday lives is to be obedient to its principles. In (John 14:23) Jesus said, "Anyone who loves me will obey my teaching. My Father will love them, and we will come to them and make our home with them." By obeying God's Word, we show our love for God and experience His blessings.

The Bible is the foundation of our faith, and the primary way God reveals Himself to us. It is our source of spiritual nourishment and growth and the way we develop a deeper relationship with God. By reading, studying, and applying God's word to our daily lives, we can experience its benefits and blessings. (Psalm 119:105) says, "Your word is a lamp for my feet, a light on my path."

Regularly reading the Bible provides numerous benefits for your life.

It brings us closer to God. Reading the Bible teaches us more about God's character and will for our lives, which helps us develop a deeper relationship with Him.

It provides us with wisdom and guidance. The Bible contains many stories and teachings to help us navigate life's challenges and make wise decisions.

Reading stories of God's faithfulness and love gives us hope and encouragement during difficult times. The Bible is filled with such stories.

It helps us understand our purpose. Reading the Bible can help us better understand our purpose in life and what God has called us to do.

The Bible teaches us to love others, God, and our neighbors as ourselves. By reading the Bible, we can learn to love others more deeply.

It helps us grow in our faith. Regularly reading the Bible can aid in our spiritual growth and lead us to become more Christ-like.

It brings joy and peace to our lives. The Bible contains many promises of happiness and peace for believers. Reading these promises helps us experience more Joy and peace daily.

CHAPTER 5

Baptism In The Holy Spirit

An Experience that Brings Transformation

Embarking on the journey of receiving the Baptism in the Holy Spirit is a profound and transforming step in the life of a Christian. This experience is not just a ritual or tradition but an invitation to connect with the Holy Spirit on a deeper level. In the waters of baptism, we die to our old selves, and by receiving the Baptism in the Holy Spirit, we rise anew, empowered by God's Spirit dwelling within us.

The baptism of the Holy Spirit is a profound experience that occurs when the Spirit of God comes upon a believer. It is not just a theological concept but a personal encounter that fills the believer's mind with a genuine understanding of the scriptures. The Holy Spirit imparts spiritual gifts that empower believers for service in the body of Christ. After receiving the gift of the Holy Spirit, we are filled with a greater desire to surrender to God's guidance and allow His Spirit to work within us, transforming our hearts, minds, and spirits.

After receiving the Holy Spirit, anticipate a heightened awareness of God's love and a deepening of your spiritual gifts. So, as you pray for the Baptism in the Holy Spirit, do so with great expectation and a heart open to God's transforming power. This encounter will be a defining moment in your spiritual journey, propelling you into a deeper, more intimate relationship with the One who breathes life into your being.

Baptism in the Holy Spirit is a separate and distinct experience from salvation and water baptism. The Apostle Peter referred to it as the gift of the Holy Spirit. It is a common misconception that the gift of the Holy Spirit was only given to the 120 individuals present in the upper room. However, in Acts 2, Peter clarifies that this gift is intended for every Christian.

Then Peter said unto them, Peter replied, "Each of you must repent of your sins and turn to God, and be baptized in the name of Jesus Christ for the forgiveness of your sins. Then you will receive the gift of the Holy Spirit. [39] This promise is to you, to your children, and to those far away[a]—all who have been called by the Lord our God." (Acts 2:38-39) NLT:

As Jesus drew near the end of his earthly ministry and drew closer to his crucifixion, he told the disciples he would not leave them comfortless but would send the Holy Spirit to them.

(John. 14:16). I will ask the Father, and he will give you another comforter who will never leave you.

Vs.17 He is the Holy Spirit, who leads into all truth. The world cannot receive him because it isn't looking for him and doesn't recognize him. But you know him because he lives with you now and later will be in you.

After His resurrection, Jesus commanded his disciples not to begin public ministry until they received the Holy Spirit's baptism. He instructed them not to leave Jerusalem but to wait for the Promise of the Father, which they had heard from Him. John had baptized them with water, but they would be baptized with the Holy Spirit not many days from then.

"And now I will send the Holy Spirit, just as my Father promised. But stay here in the city until the Holy Spirit comes and fills you with power from Heaven." (Luke 24:49)

Jesus emphasized the need to wait on the Holy Spirit to be empowered for service.

"You shall receive power when the Holy Spirit has come upon you, and you shall be witnesses to me in Jerusalem, and in all Judea and Samaria, and to the end of the earth. "(Acts 1:8)

The account of the baptism of the Holy Spirit in (Acts 2:1-4) is a significant event in the early church. It signifies the fulfillment of Jesus' promise to baptize His followers with the Holy Spirit. After Jesus ascended into heaven, the disciples and others, totaling 120 people, gathered in an upper room. They were there, waiting for the promised Holy Spirit. On the Day of Pentecost. While they were all together in one place, suddenly, there was a sound of rushing wind filling the room, a symbol of the power and movement of the Holy Spirit. At this moment, I'm sure their voices were raised with passion and conviction, creating a symphony of praise as they witnessed this miraculous event. Again, they were filled with awe and wonder as tongues of fire rested upon each of their heads, signaling the arrival of the Holy Spirit.

They were filled with the Holy Spirit and began to speak in other tongues as the Spirit enabled them. The sight of people speaking in different languages and understanding each other was almost unbelievable, yet it was happening.

The miraculous event of the 120 speaking in tongues drew a crowd of devout Jews from every nation under heaven who were in Jerusalem at that time for the Feast of Pentecost.

Astonished and bewildered, the crowd heard the disciples speaking in their native languages, declaring the wonders of God. Some were amazed, while others were perplexed, wondering how these Galileans could speak in languages they had never learned. Peter, filled with boldness and the power of the Holy Spirit, stood up with the eleven disciples and addressed the crowd. He explained to them that what they were witnessing was the fulfillment of Joel's prophecy, which had foretold that in the last days, God would pour out His Spirit on all people. (Joel 2:28)

Peter boldly proclaimed the message of Jesus Christ, testifying to His life, death, and resurrection, and calling the people to repentance and faith in Him for the forgiveness of sins. He declared, "Repent and be baptized, every one of you, in the name of Jesus Christ for the forgiveness of your sins. And you will receive the gift of the Holy Spirit." (Acts 2:38) NIV:

Many who heard Peter's message were deeply convicted by the Holy Spirit and responded with repentance and faith. About three thousand people were baptized that day, joining the early Christian community, and becoming part of the body of believers.

The baptism in the Holy Spirit at Pentecost marked the birth of the church and inaugurated a new era of God's redemptive work in the world. It empowered the disciples to proclaim the gospel message boldly and to carry out the mission that Jesus had entrusted to them. It also demonstrated the universality of the gospel, as people from every nation and language were included in God's plan of salvation.

The events of Pentecost continue to inspire and encourage believers today. They remind us of the transforming power of the Holy Spirit and the importance of being filled with The Holy Spirit for effective ministry and witness.

Once you have accepted Christ, you can rest assured that the Holy Spirit is always with you, ready to fill you with His Spirit, provide you with His power, and equip you with spiritual gifts for ministry. God has already given the Holy Spirit to you. He sent the Holy Spirit into the world on the day of Pentecost.

Now, it is up to you to ask for and receive this precious gift of the Holy Spirit. It's unnecessary to plead with God to grant you the gift, for He has already been given. You can receive Him in the same way you received Jesus through faith. Just ask Him to enter your Spirit and fill you with His Spirit. Jesus tells us how to receive the Holy Spirit in Luke chapter eleven.

Jesus was talking about a son asking his Father for something. You are a child of God; he is your Father.

"If a son shall ask bread of any of you that is a father, will he give him a stone? Or if he ask a fish, will he for a fish give him a serpent? Or if he shall ask an egg, will he offer him a scorpion?" If ye then, being evil, know how to give good gifts unto your children: how much more shall your heavenly Father give the Holy Spirit to them that ask him? (Lu.11:11-13)

God desires all of us to be filled with the Holy Spirit, but our will is involved in receiving. Just as in being born again, God will not force you to receive the Gift of the Holy Spirit; He gives us but gives us an invitation to accept. Our part is to ask and receive by faith. Humble ourselves before God, and be willing to give him our whole Spirit, soul, and body by surrendering our will to His. Then, we can ask God to fill us with the Holy Spirit and expect to receive when we ask.

Many signs follow this gift, one of which is speaking in tongues, a language you have not learned.

Some Christians believe that speaking in a language you have not learned is a sign that accompanies the baptism in the Holy Spirit, based primarily on passages such as (Acts 2:4), where the disciples spoke in tongues when they were filled with the Holy Spirit on the Day of Pentecost.

On the other hand, others believe one of the other spiritual gifts, such as those listed in (1 Corinthians 12:4-11) may be bestowed on a believer instead of speaking in tongues.

Ultimately, Christians with different views on this issue can still agree on the fundamental importance of being filled with the Holy Spirit and allowing His presence and power to transform their lives and empower them for ministry.

Through our faith, we can receive the Gift of the Holy Spirit and other spiritual gifts he has chosen to bestow on us to enhance our ability to minister to others.

When you receive the Holy Spirit, he lives in you as your Comforter, Counselor, Helper, Intercessor,

Advocate, Strength, and Teacher. He will assist you in every aspect of your Christian life. The more you rely on Him, the more strength you'll find to resist Satan's temptations. Since prayer and reading God's word are the primary ways God speaks to us, you will have a greater desire to read your Bible and pray.

Being filled with the Holy Spirit has many benefits for believers. Before I move on to the next chapter, I will summarize just a few.

1. Empowerment for ministry: When believers are filled with the Holy Spirit, they receive the power to witness and minister to others effectively. The Holy Spirit equips us with spiritual gifts to serve and build up the body of Christ.

2. Guidance and direction: The Holy Spirit guides us in all truth and helps us discern God's will for our lives. He also gives us wisdom and understanding to make wise decisions.

3. Comfort and peace: The Holy Spirit is our comforter and brings us peace in times of trouble. He comforts us with God's love and helps us overcome fear and anxiety.

4. Spiritual growth and maturity: The Holy Spirit helps us grow spiritually and become more like Christ. He produces the fruit of the Spirit in our lives, such as love, joy, peace, patience, kindness, goodness, faithfulness, gentleness, and self-control.

5. Protection and deliverance: The Holy Spirit protects us from spiritual attacks and delivers us from evil. He gives us the strength to resist temptation and overcome sin.

6. Fellowship with God: The Holy Spirit enables a deep and intimate relationship with God. He helps us pray and worship in Spirit and truth and gives us access to the Father through Jesus Christ.

Overall, being filled with the Holy Spirit is essential for Christians to live victorious lives.

CHAPTER SIX

The Power Of Giving

Embracing a Life of Generosity

For Christians, giving is a powerful act that showcases their deep love and unwavering commitment to serving God. It is an expression of genuine empathy and compassion towards those in need. By giving, we honor not only our faith but also the teachings of Christ himself, demonstrating our devotion and obedience to his message of selflessness and generosity.

When we give, we imitate Christ's selfless nature, who gave us His life. Through our generosity, we experience the joy of being part of God's divine plan to bless others and advance His kingdom. By giving to others, we position ourselves to receive God's abundant blessings.

The apostle Paul said in (Acts 20:35), "I have shown you in every way, by laboring like this, that you must support the weak. And remember the words of the Lord Jesus, that He said, 'It is more blessed to give than to receive.'

"One of the primary ways Satan attacks a believer is through their finances. But when we give God control of our finances, we enter a financial partnership with Him. When we surrender our finances to God, our blessings flow from above. (James 1:17) says, "Every good gift and every perfect gift is from above and comes down from the Father of lights, with whom there is no variation."

(Deuteronomy 8:18 says), "And you shall remember the LORD your God, for it is He who gives you the power to get wealth that He may establish His covenant which He swore to your fathers, as it is this day."

God wants us to enjoy the good things in this life; He delights in His children to be blessed. However, He does not bless us financially to consume it all on ourselves. He blesses us so we can be a blessing to others and support the mission and ministry of Christ and his kingdom. God provides us with financial blessings, and In return, all He asks is that we give a small portion of our income to Him. One of the ways we do this is by giving the tithe, which means "one-tenth" of our income. Tithing is recorded as far back as Genesis and has been honored throughout the church age. In fact, God says the tithe does not belong to us but is His. When we hold back tithes and offerings from God, He calls it robbery.

(Malachi 3:8-10) says, "Will a man rob God? Yet you have robbed Me! But you say, 'In what way have we robbed You?' In tithes and offerings... Bring all the tithes into the Storehouse, that there may be food in My house, and try Me now in this," says the LORD of hosts, "If I will not open for you the windows of heaven and pour out for you such blessing that there will not be room enough to receive it."

God's blessings always follow obedience. When we obey God's commandment to tithe and give offerings, He promises to open windows from Heaven and pour out His blessing on us. There are heavenly blessings in God's storehouse just waiting to be released through our obedient giving.

According to scripture, tithes should be given to the local church. God's word instructs us to bring our tithe to the Storehouse, which is the place where we worship and feast on God's word. For example, we don't eat at McDonald's and then go to Burger King to pay; we pay where we eat. We should pay our tithe where we are spiritually fed.

Giving is putting God first. Jesus said, "But seek first the kingdom of God and His righteousness, and all these things shall be added to you.

(Matthew 6:33) Says, When you honor God with a tenth of your income, He makes sure that all of your needs are met according to his riches in Heaven.

(Luke 6:38) says, Give, and it shall be given unto you; good measure, pressed down, and shaken together, and running over, shall men give into your bosom. For with the same measure that ye mete withal, it shall be measured to you again. Giving generously releases God's generosity into your life.

Not only does generous giving activate His blessings, but it also keeps us from becoming self-centered. Giving demonstrates our reliance on God and our gratitude for His love. In return, He showers us with countless blessings, demonstrating His love for us. Imagine the incredible impact it would have on the world if every Christian gave generously of their time, talents, and finances. There would be an abundance of resources to reach the entire world with the message of Christ and to meet the needs of the poor. God's word says what we sow is what we reap. Therefore, if we sow generously, we will reap generously, and if we sow sparingly, we will reap sparingly. (2 Corinthians 9:6-7) To live a life of generosity, we must be generous givers.

In the book of Genesis, we encounter a significant moment in Jacob's life. He makes a solemn promise to tithe a tenth of everything he had to God. This act of faithfulness, as we later see, led to numerous blessings from God. One such instance is recorded in (Genesis 32:10) when Jacob, facing a dire situation, prays to God for deliverance. He reminds God of his promise to tithe a tenth, and in response, God blesses him with protection, provision, and favor. This powerful example underscores how God rewards those who are faithful in giving and stewardship. By trusting in God and prioritizing Him, we can experience His blessings in ways we never imagined.

Perhaps Jacob learned generosity from his Father, Isaac.

(Gen 26:12-14) Then Isaac sowed in that land, and received in the same year an hundredfold: and the Lord blessed him. And the man waxed great, and went forward, and grew until he became very great: For he had possession of flocks, and possession of herds, and great store of servants: and the Philistines envied him.

As a result of Jacob's obedience to give God a tithe of all he had, God set a chain of events in motion that brought even more blessings and favor into Jacobs's life, despite his uncle Laban changing his wages ten times. This demonstrates that no matter how hard someone tries to hold you back, God makes a way where there seems to be no way,

Fulfillment of the Covenant:

God made a covenant with Abraham, Jacob's grandfather, promising to bless his descendants and make them a great nation. This covenant, a testament to God's faithfulness, was passed down to Isaac, Jacob's father, and then to Jacob himself (Genesis 28:13-15). Jacob's financial blessings can be seen as a direct fulfillment of God's covenant promises to Abraham and his descendants.

When reading about the covenant God made Abraham, don't forget that you are also included in the Abrahamic blessing through Christ.

(Galatians 3:29) NIV: If you belong to Christ, then you are Abraham's seed and heirs according to the promise.

Throughout Jacob's life, there are instances where God intervened and guided him. For example, when Jacob worked for his uncle Laban, God directed him to selectively breed the flocks, significantly increasing his wealth. (Genesis 30:25-43) This demonstrates God's involvement in Jacob's affairs and a manifestation of His promise to prosper him.

Testing and Transformation:

Jacob's life was marked by various trials and challenges, including his dealings with Laban and his estrangement from his brother Esau. These experiences transformed Jacob's character. God often uses challenges and adversity to refine us. When life seems unfair, don't get bitter; get better.

Repentance and Seeking God:

Before Jacob returned to his homeland, he had a pivotal encounter with God at Peniel. (Genesis 32:22-32) In this encounter, Jacob wrestled with God, resulting in a change of his name to Israel, signifying a transformation of character.

Jacob's willingness to confront his past and seek reconciliation with his estranged brother Esau demonstrated repentance and a desire to align with God's will.

Faith and Trust in God:

Jacob demonstrated faith and trust in God throughout his life. Although his journey included moments of uncertainty and fear, he consistently acknowledged God's presence and sought His guidance. The financial blessings can be seen as a reward for Jacob's trust and reliance on God during life's challenges.

Let me summarize this chapter on generosity and provide you with seven key takeaways.

1. Abundance: Giving generously will bring abundance into your life, not just financially but in all areas.

2. Joy: Giving generously brings joy and happiness to both the giver and the receiver, which is a double blessing.

3. Blessings from God: Giving generously shows your faith and trust in God, and He promises to bless those who give.

4. Peace: Giving generously can bring peace of mind, knowing that you are helping others and positively impacting the world.

5. Gratitude: Giving generously can help you cultivate a sense of gratitude for all the blessings in your life.

6. Goodwill: Giving generously can help you build goodwill and positive relationships with others,

bringing blessings through new opportunities and connections.

7. Spiritual growth: Giving generously can be a way to grow spiritually as you learn to let go of attachment to material possessions and focus on more meaningful aspects of life.

Do you want God's best? Then, I challenge you to give generously of your tithes, offerings, time, and energy.

CHAPTER 7

SPIRITUAL GIFTS
ROMANS 12:6-8

Discover and Employ Your Spiritual Gifts

In This Chapter, we are going to delve into the Christian experience on a deeper level. Once you have learned the basics and established a good foundation, the next step is to begin ministering to others. By this time, you have more than likely discovered your motivational Gift (also known as Service Gift) and are ready to use it to bless others.

You can be assured that the Holy Spirit has anointed and equipped you to serve in that area and will be there to help you succeed.

(Hebrews 6:1-3) NLT:

So, let us stop going over the basic teachings about Christ again and again. Let us go on instead and become mature in our understanding. Indeed, we don't need to start again with the fundamental importance of repenting from evil deeds[a] and placing our faith in God. You don't need further instruction about baptisms, the laying on of hands, the resurrection of the dead, and eternal judgment. And so, God willing, we will move forward to further understanding.

Discovering and embracing our spiritual gifts is not just a theological concept; it's a deeply personal journey that shapes our identity, purpose, and impact on the world. As believers, God uniquely designed and equipped us to fulfill His purposes and advance His kingdom.

My aim is to assist you in your gift to Serve, which will guide you towards a fulfilling role in ministry. Through our journey, we will thoroughly explore the seven motivational gifts described in Romans 12 and how they manifest in our lives.

After learning about each gift, you can determine what resonates most. The Holy Spirit grants us these gifts and instills a passion within us to use them for His purposes.

Along with the seven motivational gifts of serving, the New Testament mentions other spiritual gifts bestowed by the Holy Spirit. These will be listed at the end of this chapter. Furthermore, there are additional gifts given by the Holy Spirit that may not be explicitly mentioned in the Bible but are vital for the body of Christ and divinely anointed for ministry.

God has fearfully and wonderfully made each of us, giving us specific gifts and abilities that reflect His image and purposes. Our spiritual gifts are not accidental or incidental but intentional expressions of God's grace and love towards us. Recognizing and embracing our unique design enables us to walk confidently in our calling and identity as beloved children of God.

Just as physical DNA determines our biological traits and characteristics, our spiritual gifts reveal the unique imprint of God's Spirit upon our lives. Discovering our spiritual gifts is like uncovering hidden treasures within ourselves – treasures that possess the transformative power to change lives, communities, and even nations. Each gift carries a sacred responsibility and opportunity to make a significant difference.

Our spiritual gifts connect us to a larger narrative – God's story of redemption and restoration. As we discern and cultivate our gifts, we actively participate in God's unfolding plan to reconcile all things to Himself. Our gifts are not meant to be hoarded or hidden but shared generously for the common good, bearing witness to the transforming power of God's love in our lives and the world.

Discovering and utilizing our spiritual gifts is not just about personal fulfillment; it's about building authentic community and relationships. Our gifts are not meant to be hoarded or hidden but shared generously for the common good, bearing witness to the transforming power of God's love in our lives and the world. By embracing our gifts and affirming the gifts of others, we develop a culture of honor, mutual respect, and collaboration that reflects the heart of God. At the heart of our spiritual journey lies a profound truth: our lives matter, and our gifts have eternal significance. As we faithfully steward the gifts entrusted to us, we become God's agents of transformation and reconciliation in a broken and hurting world. Our acts of service, encouragement, and expressions of love ripple outward, leaving a lasting legacy that points others to hope and healing in Christ.

Discovering and embracing our spiritual gifts is not always easy, but it is undoubtedly worth the effort. It is a journey of self-discovery, growth, and empowerment, guided by the gentle hand of the Holy Spirit. May we embrace this journey with open hearts and willing spirits, trusting that God will use our gifts to bring glory to His name and to bless the lives of those around us.

The First Gift Mentioned In Romans 12

Is The Gift Of Prophecy.

(Ro. 12:6) In his grace, God has given us different gifts for doing certain things well. "So, if God has given you the ability to prophesy, speak out with as much faith as God has given you."

In the realm of spiritual gifts, the ability to prophesy provides divine revelation and insight into the body of Christ.

Often misunderstood or underutilized, prophecy remains a powerful tool for edification, comfort, encouragement, and alignment with God's purposes. Let's explore the nature of the gift of prophecy, its significance in the believer's life, and how we can cultivate and deploy this gift in service to the kingdom.

At its core, the gift of prophecy involves receiving and communicating messages from God. It goes beyond mere prediction of future events, encompassing a broader spectrum of spiritual insights, moral guidance, and divine revelation. Prophets throughout Scripture served as mouthpieces for God, delivering His word with boldness, clarity, and authority. In today's context, prophecy reveals God's heart, aligns believers with His will, and calls them to deeper intimacy and obedience. Within the body of Christ, the gift of prophecy plays a crucial role in building up the community of believers. It serves as a catalyst for spiritual growth, awakening hearts to the reality of God's presence and His purposes for His people.

Prophecy brings correction, encouragement, and direction, helping individuals and congregations to align with God's plans and pursue His kingdom agenda. Moreover, prophecy fosters a culture of expectancy and faith, where believers eagerly anticipate God's voice and respond obediently to His leading.

While the gift of prophecy is a supernatural endowment from the Holy Spirit, it requires cultivation and stewardship on the part of the believer. Developing the gift involves deepening one's relationship with God through prayer, worship, and meditation on His Word. It requires sensitivity to the prompting of the Holy Spirit and a willingness to step out in faith, trusting God to speak through us. Additionally, prophetic training, mentorship, and accountability can provide valuable guidance and support as we seek to grow in the exercise of this gift. As vessels of God's prophetic word, we are called to steward this gift for the glory of His name and the advancement of His kingdom. We serve the kingdom by speaking God's truth with boldness and compassion, confronting sin, and calling others to repentance and reconciliation. We offer hope and encouragement to the weary and oppressed, pointing them to the promises of God and His faithfulness to fulfill them. Moreover, prophecy equips and mobilizes believers for mission and ministry, empowering them to walk in obedience and fulfill their God-given calling.

The gift of prophecy remains a precious and indispensable tool in the arsenal of spiritual gifts bestowed upon the church. As we embrace this gift with humility and reverence, we open ourselves to the transformative power of God's word in our lives and the lives of others. Let us seek to cultivate and deploy the gift of prophecy with wisdom and discernment, always mindful of our responsibility to speak truth in love and to glorify God in all that we do.

The Second Gift Is The Gift Of Service.

(Romans 12:7) If your gift is serving others, serve them well.

The gift of Service, which is also known as the gift of ministry, is an amazing example of selflessness and compassion. Rooted in the example of Jesus Christ, who came not to be served but to serve, this gift empowers believers to meet practical needs and minister to others with humility and love. Let us also delve into the nature of the gift of service, its significance in the body of Christ, and how we can cultivate and deploy this gift to serve the kingdom.

The gift of service is characterized by a willingness to sacrificially invest time, resources, and energy in meeting the needs of others. It encompasses a wide range of practical tasks and acts of kindness, from serving meals to the homeless to offering a listening ear to the hurting. Those with this gift have a servant's heart, finding joy and fulfillment in serving others behind the scenes, often without seeking recognition or reward.

Within the body of Christ, the gift of service plays a vital role in fostering community, unity, and mutual care. It is the glue that holds the body together as believers use their gifts and talents to minister to one another in love. Service creates a culture of generosity and hospitality, where each member is valued and affirmed for their unique contributions. Moreover, service opens doors for evangelism and outreach, as acts of kindness and compassion pave the way for sharing the gospel and making disciples.

While the gift of service is often innate, it can be cultivated and developed through intentional practice and discipleship. Developing the gift involves cultivating a servant's heart, following the example of Jesus, who washed His disciples' feet and laid down His life for others. It requires sensitivity to the needs of those around us and a willingness to step out of our comfort zones to meet those needs. Additionally, serving alongside others in the body of Christ provides opportunities for growth and mutual encouragement as we learn from one another and bear one another's burdens.

As stewards of the gift of service, we are called to serve the kingdom by ministering to the physical, emotional, and spiritual needs of others. We serve by feeding the hungry, clothing the naked, and visiting the sick and imprisoned. We serve by offering a helping hand to the weary and burdened, providing practical assistance and emotional support. Moreover, we serve by using our gifts and talents to build up the body of Christ, whether through hospitality, administration, or acts of mercy and compassion.

The gift of service is a testament to the transformative power of love and selflessness in the kingdom of God. As we embrace this gift with humility and obedience, we become channels of God's grace and compassion in a hurting and broken world. Let us cultivate and deploy the gift of service with joy and gratitude, knowing that we are serving Christ in serving others. (Matthew 25:40)

The Third Gift Is The Gift Of Teaching:

(Romans. 12:7b) If you are a teacher, teach well.

In the intricate design of spiritual abilities, the gift of teaching reveals God's teachings and guides believers on their faith journey.

Rooted in a passion for studying and sharing Scripture, this gift empowers believers to communicate God's truth with clarity, creativity, and relevance. In this overview, we will explore the nature of the gift of teaching, its significance in the body of Christ, and how we can cultivate and deploy this gift to serve the kingdom.

The ability to communicate God's truth through teaching can transform lives by engaging the mind and stirring the heart. It goes beyond simply sharing information; it aims to inspire and equip believers for faithful living and ministry. Those with this gift have a hunger for studying Scripture, a knack for making complex concepts understandable, and a passion for helping others grow in their relationship with God.

Within the body of Christ, the gift of teaching plays a vital role in nurturing spiritual growth, fostering biblical literacy, and equipping believers for ministry. Through teaching, believers are grounded in the foundational truths of the faith, equipped to discern truth from error, and empowered to live out their faith in their daily lives. Moreover, teaching creates a culture of discipleship and accountability, where believers are encouraged to grow in their knowledge and understanding of God's Word.

While the gift of teaching may have existed in one from birth, it can be cultivated and developed through intentional study, practice, and mentorship. Developing the gift involves deepening one's understanding of Scripture, honing one's communication skills, and seeking feedback and guidance from seasoned teachers and leaders. It requires a commitment to lifelong learning and growth and a willingness to step out in faith and take on opportunities for teaching and leadership within the church.

As stewards of the gift of teaching, we are called to serve the kingdom by proclaiming God's truth with boldness and clarity, equipping believers for ministry and mission, and guiding them on the path of discipleship. We serve by making the Word of God accessible and applicable to people's lives, helping them to understand its relevance to their everyday experiences and challenges. Moreover, we serve by fostering a culture of learning and growth within the body of Christ, where believers are encouraged to ask questions, wrestle with complex concepts, and grow in their faith.

The gift of teaching is a precious and indispensable tool in the arsenal of spiritual gifts bestowed upon the church. As we embrace this gift with humility and diligence, we become instruments of God's grace and truth, guiding others on the journey of faith and discipleship. Let us cultivate and deploy the gift of teaching with wisdom and discernment, always mindful of our responsibility to accurately handle the Word of truth (2 Timothy 2:15) and to point others to the One who is the Way, the Truth, and the Life (John 14:6).

Next Is The Gift Of Exhortation

Embracing the Call to Lift Others Up

(Romans 12:8) If your gift is to encourage others, be encouraging.

The ability to give encouragement is a valuable spiritual gift that can provide hope and motivation to individuals who may be facing challenges or adversity. Rooted in a deep sense of empathy and compassion, this gift empowers believers to uplift and motivate others to pursue God's purposes with renewed faith and zeal. In this teaching, it's essential to understand the nature of the gift of exhortation, its significance in the body of Christ, and how this gift can be used in service to the kingdom.

The gift of exhortation is characterized by the ability to offer encouragement, comfort, and motivation to those struggling or in need. It goes beyond mere positivity or cheerfulness, delving into the realm of spiritual discernment and divine insight. Those with this gift have a keen sense of empathy and understanding, knowing how to speak words that uplift the soul and inspire others to press forward in their faith journey.

Within the body of Christ, the gift of exhortation plays a vital role in fostering resilience, perseverance, and spiritual growth It serves as a beacon of hope in times of trial and adversity, offering comfort and assurance to the weary and oppressed. Exhortation also serves as a catalyst for transformation, challenging believers to step out in faith, pursue their calling, and make a difference in the world. Moreover, exhortation fosters unity and community within the body, creating a culture of encouragement and mutual support.

While the gift of exhortation may come naturally to some, it can be cultivated and developed through intentional practice and discipleship. Developing the gift involves deepening one's relationship with God through prayer, worship, and meditation on His Word. It requires sensitivity to the leading of the Holy Spirit and a willingness to step out in faith, trusting God to use our words to minister to others. Additionally, surrounding ourselves with a community of believers who can offer accountability, feedback, and support can help us grow in exercising this gift.

As stewards of the gift of exhortation, we are called to serve the kingdom by offering hope, comfort, and support to those who are struggling or in need. We serve by speaking words of encouragement and affirmation, reminding others of God's faithfulness and His promises. We serve alongside the broken and the hurt, offering a listening ear and a compassionate heart. Moreover, we serve by challenging and motivating believers to live out their faith with boldness and courage, knowing that God is with them every step of the way.

The gift of exhortation stands as a beacon of light in a dark and broken world. As we embrace this gift with humility and obedience, we become channels of God's grace and compassion, bringing hope and healing to those around us. Let us cultivate and deploy the gift of exhortation with wisdom and discernment, always mindful of our responsibility to speak truth in love and glorify God in all we do.

The Fifth is The Gift Of Giving:

Sharing God's Blessings with Generosity

(Romans 12:8) If it is giving, give generously.

Within the spectrum of spiritual gifts, the gift of giving is a testament to God's generous nature and

His desire for His children to emulate that generosity. This gift, rooted deeply in the teachings of Christ and the early church, is a divine endowment bestowed upon believers to share their resources with others joyfully. A spirit of generosity and stewardship characterizes the gift of giving. It recognizes that all we have belongs to God and is to be used for His glory. It involves sharing our financial, material, or relational resources with others out of a heart of love and compassion. Those with this gift find joy and fulfillment in giving, knowing that their generosity has the power to bless and transform lives.

Within the body of Christ, the gift of giving plays a vital role in supporting the church's work, meeting the needs of the poor and marginalized, and advancing the gospel locally and globally. It serves as a tangible expression of God's love and provision, providing for the material needs of individuals and communities. Giving also fosters unity and community within the body, as believers share in the joy of giving and receiving together.

While the gift of giving may come naturally to some, it can be cultivated and developed through intentional practice and discipleship. Developing the gift involves cultivating a heart of generosity and stewardship, recognizing that all we have is a gift from God to be used for His purposes. It requires prayerful discernment and obedience to the leading of the Holy Spirit as we seek opportunities to give cheerfully and sacrificially. Additionally, surrounding ourselves with a community of believers who model and encourage a lifestyle of generosity can help us to grow in the exercise of this gift.

As stewards of the gift of giving, we are called to serve the kingdom by sharing our resources generously and sacrificially to advance God's purposes. We serve by supporting ministries, missions, and charitable causes that align with God's heart and priorities. We serve by meeting the practical needs of those around us through financial assistance, material provision, or acts of kindness and hospitality. Moreover, we serve by giving with a cheerful heart and a spirit of gratitude, knowing that our generosity can bless and transform lives for eternity. As we embrace this gift with humility and obedience, we become channels of God's love and provision, bringing hope and healing to a hurting world.

The Sixth Gift of Serving Is Leadership:

Guiding Others with Vision and Integrity

(Romans 12:8) If God has given you leadership ability, take the responsibility seriously.

Within the array of spiritual gifts, leadership's gift offers direction and motivation to those who have been bestowed with it. This gift empowers believers to guide, inspire, and influence others toward a shared vision or goal.

The gift of leadership is characterized by the ability to provide vision, direction, and guidance to others. It involves shepherding and empowering individuals or groups to achieve a shared purpose or mission. Those with this gift possess qualities such as vision, wisdom, discernment, and integrity. They lead by example, serving others with humility and grace. Within the body of Christ, the gift of leadership plays a crucial role in guiding and equipping believers for ministry and mission. It provides stability and direction, fostering unity and collaboration among diverse members of the body. Leadership creates an environment where individuals are empowered to discover and deploy their gifts and talents for the glory of God.

Moreover, leadership mobilizes the church for effective evangelism and discipleship, enabling believers to fulfill the Great Commission and make disciples of all nations.

While the gift of leadership may come naturally to some, developing it involves growing in character and competency, deepening one's relationship with God, and dependence on the Holy Spirit. It requires humility, self-awareness, and a willingness to learn from both successes and failures. Additionally, leadership training, coaching, and accountability can provide valuable support and guidance as we seek to grow in the exercise of this gift.

As stewards of the gift of leadership, we are called to serve the kingdom by providing vision, direction, and guidance to others. We serve by casting a compelling vision for ministry and mission, inspiring others to join God's redemptive work. We serve by equipping and empowering believers for ministry, helping them discover and effectively deploy their gifts and talents. Moreover, we serve by fostering unity and collaboration within the body of Christ, creating an environment where all members are valued and affirmed for their unique contributions. We become catalysts for change and transformation as we embrace this gift with humility and obedience. Let us cultivate and deploy the gift of leadership with wisdom and discernment, always mindful of our responsibility to steward God's people for His glory and the advancement of His kingdom.

The Last Serving Gift Mentioned In Romans 12

Is The Gift Of Mercy:

Extending Compassion and Grace

(Romans 12:8) If it is to show mercy, do it cheerfully.

This gift empowers believers to show compassion, empathy, and kindness to those suffering or in need. The gift of mercy is characterized by a deep sensitivity to the pain and suffering of others and a willingness to extend grace and compassion to those who are hurting. It involves showing kindness, forgiveness, and understanding to those who need comfort and support. Those with this gift have a tender heart and a willingness to come alongside others in their time of need, offering a listening ear, a shoulder to cry on, and practical assistance.

Within the body of Christ, the gift of mercy plays a vital role in ministering to the broken, the hurting, and the marginalized. It offers comfort and healing, bringing hope and restoration to those in pain and despair. Mercy creates a culture of grace and forgiveness, where we can experience the unconditional love of God and find healing and wholeness. Moreover, mercy bridges the gap between different members of the body, fostering unity and compassion within the church.

Developing the gift involves deepening one's relationship with God and growing in compassion and empathy for others. It requires a willingness to step out of our comfort zones and experience the pain and suffering of those around us. Additionally, surrounding ourselves with a community of believers who model and encourage a lifestyle of mercy and compassion can help us grow in this gift as stewards of the gift of mercy; we are called to serve the kingdom by ministering to the broken, the hurting, and the marginalized. We serve by offering a listening ear and a compassionate heart to those who need comfort and support. We serve by showing kindness, forgiveness, and understanding to those who are struggling with sin, addiction, or brokenness. Moreover, we serve by advocating for justice and mercy in our communities, standing up for the oppressed and marginalized, and working toward healing and reconciliation.

As we embrace this gift with humility and obedience, we become channels of God's love and compassion, bringing hope and healing to a hurting world. Let us cultivate and deploy the gift of mercy with wisdom and discernment, always mindful of our responsibility to show kindness, forgiveness, and grace to all those around us.

Seven Ways To Discover Your Spiritual Gift.

Discovering your spiritual gifts is a deeply personal and enriching journey that requires sincere introspection and openness to God's guidance. Here's how you might approach it:

1. Prayerful Reflection: Set aside dedicated time in prayer, inviting God into your discernment process. Humbly ask Him to reveal your spiritual gifts, recognizing that He knows you intimately and desires to equip you for His service.

2. Soul Search: Reflect on your life experiences, passions, and talents. Consider the activities that bring you the greatest sense of fulfillment and joy. These inclinations often provide clues to your spiritual gifts, reflecting God's unique design for you.

3. Dive into Scripture: Immerse yourself in God's Word, particularly passages that discuss spiritual gifts. As you meditate on verses like Romans 12:6-8 and 1 Corinthians 12, ask God to illuminate His truth and show you how it applies to your life.

4. Seek Wise Counsel: Ask trusted mentors, friends, or fellow believers for insight. Their observations and feedback can offer valuable perspectives that may confirm or shed light on your areas of gifting.

5. Hands-on Exploration: Engage in various ministries or volunteer opportunities within your church and community. As you serve others, pay attention to where you feel most alive and effective. These moments often reveal glimpses of your spiritual gifts in action.

6. Assessment Tools: To gain further clarity, consider using spiritual gifts assessment resources. While these tools are not definitive, they can serve

as helpful guides in pinpointing your strengths and areas of gifting.

7. Embrace the Journey: Remember that discovering your spiritual gifts is a process, not a one-time event. Stay open to God's leading and be willing to step out of your comfort zone as you explore new avenues of service.

Above all, trust in God's timing and provision. He delights in equipping His people for meaningful Kingdom work and will faithfully guide you as you seek to discern and deploy your spiritual gifts for His glory.

Exploring the seven motivational gifts outlined in Romans 12 unveils a beautiful diversity within the body of Christ. Each gift, whether prophecy, service, teaching, exhortation, giving, leadership, or mercy, serves as a unique expression of God's grace and provision for His people.

By discovering and developing these gifts, believers are equipped to serve the kingdom excellently and effectively. Prophecy offers divine insight and revelation, guiding believers into alignment with God's purposes. Service demonstrates Christlike humility and compassion, meeting the practical needs of others with love and grace. Teaching imparts knowledge and wisdom, equipping believers for spiritual growth and maturity. Exhortation provides encouragement and motivation, spurring believers to greater faithfulness and obedience. Giving reflects God's generous heart, providing for the needs of His people and advancing His kingdom on earth. Leadership offers vision and direction, guiding believers toward a shared mission and purpose. And mercy extends God's grace and compassion, bringing healing and restoration to the broken and hurting.

As stewards of these gifts, we are called to serve the kingdom with humility, wisdom, and love. Whether through bold proclamation, humble service, inspiring teaching, compassionate encouragement, sacrificial giving, visionary leadership, or tender mercy, each believer has a vital role in advancing God's kingdom and glorifying His name. Let us embrace our unique gifts with gratitude and obedience, knowing that as we serve faithfully, we participate in unfolding God's redemptive plan for the world. May the diverse gifts of the Spirit continue to empower and unite the body of Christ, bringing glory to God and blessings to all His people.

As mentioned previously, various spiritual gifts are given to believers for ministry, along with the Motivational gifts described in Romans 12. Below is a list of these gifts for further exploration.

These gifts are listed primarily in 1 Corinthians 12 and are categorized into three main groups:

Revelation Gifts

These gifts reveal something that is hidden or unknown to the human mind.

Word of Wisdom: The ability to apply knowledge and experience to make decisions that are in accordance with God's will.

Word of Knowledge: The supernatural understanding of facts and information that could not be known through natural means.

Discerning of Spirits is the ability to discern whether a spiritual manifestation is from God, human, or demonic sources.

Power Gifts

These gifts involve the demonstration of the power of God in various ways.

Faith: Supernatural faith to believe for the impossible.

Gifts of Healings: The ability to supernaturally heal physical, emotional, or spiritual ailments.

Working of Miracles: The ability to perform extraordinary acts that defy natural laws.

Inspiration Gifts

These gifts speak to the inspired communication of God's heart and mind.

Prophecy: The ability to speak forth messages from God for edification, exhortation, and comfort.

Speaking in Tongues: The ability to speak in a language unknown to the speaker, often interpreted as a message for the church.

Interpretation of Tongues: The ability to interpret the message spoken in tongues so that the church may be edified.

Next are the categories of apostle, prophet, evangelist, pastor, and teacher, often called the "fivefold ministry" or the "fivefold gifts." This terminology is derived from (Ephesians 4:11-13) where the apostle Paul writes:

Now, these are the gifts Christ gave to the church: the apostles, the prophets, the evangelists, and the pastors and teachers. [12] Their responsibility is to equip God's people to do his work and build up the church, the body of Christ. [13] This will continue until we all come to such unity in our faith and knowledge of God's Son that we will be mature in the Lord, measuring up to the full and complete standard of Christ.

These five roles or functions within the church are foundational for equipping and edifying believers, fostering unity and maturity, and advancing the church's mission. Each ministry has a distinct focus and emphasis, yet they work together synergistically for the common goal of building up the body of Christ.

Apostle: The term "apostle" comes from the Greek word "Apostolos," meaning "one who is sent out." Apostles are often seen as pioneering leaders who are sent by God to establish new churches, preach the gospel, and lay foundations for ministry. They may also provide oversight, governance, and spiritual authority within the broader body of Christ.

Prophet: Prophets are individuals who the Holy Spirit gifts to receive and communicate divine messages, insights, and revelations. They speak forth God's word with clarity, authority, and relevance, often addressing issues of repentance, righteousness, and God's plans and purposes for His people.

Evangelist: Evangelists communicate the gospel message with passion. Their primary focus is proclaiming Christ to unbelievers and leading them to faith in Him. They often have a burden for evangelism, personal outreach, and mobilizing others for evangelistic endeavors.

Pastor: Pastors, also known as shepherds, are responsible for the care, nurture, and spiritual oversight of a local congregation or flock. They provide pastoral care, leadership, and guidance to believers, equipping them for ministry, discipleship, and spiritual growth.

Teacher: Teachers are individuals gifted in explaining and applying the truths of Scripture in a way that is understandable and relevant to others. They have a passion for biblical instruction, doctrinal clarity, and helping believers grow in their knowledge and understanding of God's word.

Together, these five ministry roles complement and support one another, contributing to the holistic health, growth, and mission of the church. They are intended to work together in harmony, diversity, and unity under the headship of Christ for the common purpose of advancing God's kingdom and glorifying His name.

These gifts are given by the Holy Spirit as He sees fit and are meant to be used for the common good of the body of Christ. They are not given for personal glory but for building up the church and advancing God's kingdom on earth.

While the traditional lists of spiritual gifts found in Scripture primarily focus on gifts related to ministry, teaching, service, and communication, some Christian traditions recognize and celebrate other forms of artistic expression and embodiment as spiritual gifts. Dance is one such example.

In some Christian contexts, dance is seen as a spiritual gift and a form of worship that can glorify

God and minister to others. Those who have the gift of dance may use movement, rhythm, and expression to convey spiritual truths, invoke the presence of God, and engage in acts of worship and praise.

The use of dance as a spiritual gift can take various forms, including:

Liturgical Dance: This involves incorporating dance into formal worship services and rituals, often in a structured and choreographed manner. Liturgical dance may be used to enhance the atmosphere of worship, illustrate biblical narratives or themes, and facilitate spiritual encounters with God.

Prophetic Dance: Prophetic dance is characterized by spontaneity, freedom of expression, and sensitivity to the Holy Spirit's leading. Those with this gift may use dance as a form of prophetic expression, conveying messages, prayers, or spiritual insights through movement and gesture.

Ministry Through Dance: Some individuals may have the gift of using dance to minister to others. This could involve performing healing, deliverance, or spiritual warfare dances or leading workshops, classes, or retreats that help others connect with God through movement and expression

Community and Celebration: Dance can also foster community, celebration, and joy within the body of Christ. Those with the gift of dance may organize social gatherings, festivals, or special events where dance is used to build relationships, express gratitude, and rejoice in God's goodness.

While dance may not be explicitly mentioned in traditional lists of spiritual gifts in Scripture, its inclusion as a form of worship and ministry is supported by biblical examples of dance as a means of praising God (e.g., Psalm 149:3; 150:4). Ultimately, the recognition of dance as a spiritual gift depends on individual interpretation and the practices of specific Christian communities.

Singing is also recognized as a form of worship and ministry that can be empowered by the Holy Spirit for the edification of the church and the glorification of God.

Here's why singing can be considered a spiritual gift:

Scriptural Support: While singing itself may not be listed as a spiritual gift, the Bible contains numerous exhortations to sing praises to God (e.g., Psalm 95:1-2; Ephesians 5:19; Colossians 3:16). Additionally, there are examples of individuals in Scripture who are noted for their musical abilities, such as King David and the Levitical singers and musicians appointed for temple worship.

Worship Leading: Singing is a central aspect of corporate worship in many Christian traditions. Those with the gift of singing may use their voices to lead congregational singing, facilitate times of prayer and adoration, and create an atmosphere conducive to encountering God's presence.

Expression of Faith: Singing can serve as a deeply personal expression of faith and devotion. Those with the gift of singing may use their voices to express love for God, proclaim His truth, and testify to His goodness and faithfulness.

Ministry and Encouragement: Singing has the power to minister to others on a spiritual and emotional level. Those with the gift of singing may use their voices to comfort the brokenhearted, encourage the discouraged, and uplift the weary through songs of hope, healing, and redemption.

Evangelism and Outreach: Singing can also be a tool for evangelism and outreach. Whether through traditional hymns, contemporary worship songs, or gospel music, singing can communicate the gospel message in a compelling and accessible way to both believers and non-believers.

In addition, Here's how artistic talents may be recognized as gifts from God: The ability to play instruments, paint, sculpt, or engage in other artistic endeavors is often recognized as talents given by God. Just as individuals are endowed with various abilities for the common good (1 Corinthians 12:4-7), artistic talents can be seen as part of God's creative design and provision for His people.

Forms of Worship: Music, visual arts, and other forms of creative expression can be powerful tools for worship and praise. Many Christians use their artistic talents to lead worship, enhance the atmosphere of corporate worship gatherings, and create visual representations of spiritual truths.

Means of Communication: Art can communicate ideas, emotions, and spiritual realities in ways that words alone cannot. Artists may use their talents to convey biblical themes, tell stories, evoke contemplation and reflection, and inspire others to draw closer to God.

Ministry and Outreach: Artists can use their talents to engage with and minister to others in various contexts. This might involve creating art for evangelistic purposes, using artistic expression as a form of therapy or healing ministry, or using creative projects to serve and bless the community.

While artistic talents may not be explicitly listed as spiritual gifts in Scripture, they are often seen as part of the broader spectrum of abilities and resources that God entrusts to His people. When used with a heart of humility, gratitude, and stewardship, these gifts can bring glory to God and contribute to the flourishing of His kingdom on earth.

All the spiritual gifts encompass a wide array of abilities and functions bestowed upon believers by the Holy Spirit for the purpose of serving others and building up the body of Christ. These gifts enable believers to fulfill various roles and ministries within the church, contributing to its growth, unity, and effectiveness in advancing God's kingdom. While some gifts involve supernatural manifestations, such as revelation, power, and inspiration, others focus on practical service, leadership, and communication. Additionally, artistic gifts, such as music, visual arts, and other forms of creative expression, are also recognized as spiritual gifts that can be used to glorify God and minister to others. Ultimately, the spiritual gifts are intended to be exercised in love, humility, and unity, under the guidance of the Holy Spirit, for the common good of the body of Christ and the fulfillment of God's purposes in the world.

Conclusion

Embracing the Future with Faith

The Christian life is a beautiful, empowering experience that brings hope, peace, and joy to those who accept it.

I encourage you to continue growing your faith and deepening your relationship with God. Do not hesitate to seek out the many available resources to assist you on your journey. Being a part of a Christian community is crucial for your spiritual growth and journey. It provides a sense of belonging, support, and accountability. Moreover, it helps you learn from others' experiences, share your own, and encourage others. As you continue to attend Church and interact with other believers, keep your focus on Christ, obey His word, and seek to serve others. Doing so can build meaningful relationships, grow your faith, and ultimately fulfill God's purpose for your life. May this book serve as a guide to help you navigate through the steps to a new beginning as a Christian. Remember, you are not alone, and God is always with you. Continue to seek Him, follow His word, and trust Him in every aspect of your life. As Philippians 1:6 says, "Being confident of this very thing, that He who has begun a good work in you will complete it until the day of Jesus Christ. Christianity is more than a mere belief system—it is a beautiful, life-changing experience that brings hope, peace, and joy to those who accept it into the depths of their hearts. As you stand at the threshold of your new beginning as a Christian, I encourage you to recognize this faith's profound impact on your life and embrace the transformative journey ahead.

The Christian walk is a continuous journey of learning and growing in your relationship with God. The Bible is the foundational guide for Christian living, "The book is a valuable source of knowledge, direction, and commitments." I implore you to immerse yourself in the Scriptures, seeking understanding and allowing the Word of God to shape your perspectives, decisions, and character. The more you delve into the richness of God's Word, the more you will discover the depths of His love and His purpose for your life.

In this journey, you are not alone. Numerous resources are available, from insightful books and online materials to local churches and mentors. Do not hesitate to ask for help or guidance when needed. Being a part of a Christian community is not just beneficial; it is crucial for your spiritual growth and journey. Surrounding yourself with fellow believers provides a sense of belonging, support, and accountability. Within the community, you can learn from others' experiences, share your own, and encourage one another along the path of faith.

As you continue to attend Church and interact with other believers, let your focus remain on Christ. He is the cornerstone of the Christian faith, the source of strength, and the ultimate example of love and service. Obey His word and seek to serve others selflessly. Through acts of kindness, you reflect Christ's love and contribute to building meaningful relationships within the community. By aligning your actions with the teachings of Christ, you not only grow in your faith but contribute to the flourishing of those around you.

As you step into this new beginning as a Christian, may God's grace abound in your life. May you experience the depth of His love, find peace in His presence, and discover joy in your relationship with Him. Your journey may have challenges, but with faith and perseverance, you will emerge stronger and more rooted in the hope that only Christ can provide. May this be the start of a life filled with purpose, love, and abundant blessings flowing from a vibrant relationship with your Heavenly Father. As you journey through life as a Christian, may God's blessings overflow abundantly upon you!

About The Author

Bob Wright is the founder and president of RestoreMeNow Ministries. With over forty years of experience as a pastor, evangelist, and mission outreach, Bob has traveled domestically and internationally, preaching and teaching the Gospel. He is a gifted speaker and author who ministers with a prophetic and healing anointing. In addition, he holds a Doctor of Ministry degree and has helped equip others to serve as pastors, evangelists, and missionaries. Bob served on the Board of Regents at Oral Roberts University and as a trustee on the board of International Charismatic Bible Ministries, a ministry founded to encourage young ministers worldwide to preach the Gospel without compromise. Bob and his wife Pam have two amazing sons, two beautiful daughters-in-law, and one fantastic grandson!

For More Information

If you want to know more about RestoreMeNow Ministries, their website, restoremenow.org, is the best place to find information about their mission, services, and upcoming events. If you have any questions or want to contact them, email them at info@restoremenow.org. Moreover, to know more about the author, you can check out the About Us section on their website.

Dear Friend,

Thank you for choosing "New Beginnings" to help guide you on your journey of exploration and growth. If you've enjoyed the insights, encouragement, and guidance offered in "New Beginnings," please take a moment to leave a review. Your words have the power to help others decide to embark on this transformative journey.

To share your review, Scan The QR Code Below. Your feedback is a gift, and I am genuinely grateful for your time and consideration.